The Best Ever Book of Sailor Jokes

*Lots and Lots of Jokes
Specially Repurposed for You-Know-Who*

Other books by Mark Young

The West Australian Joke Book
How To Promote Your Business
Dr. Young's Guide to Demotivating Employees
Guide To Selling Your Home

And about 600 other books titled:

The Best Ever Book of Jokes

To find out more, check out our websites at:

www.dolyttle.com, www.thebesteverbook.com

or visit

www.amazon.com

The Best Ever Book of Sailor Jokes

*Lots and Lots of Jokes
Specially Repurposed for You-Know-Who*

Dolyttle & Seamore
New York, New York

The Best Ever Book of Jokes: Lots and Lots of Jokes Specially Repurposed for You-Know-Who

Dolyttle & Seamore
New York, New York

© Copyright 2012. All rights reserved. No part of this book may be reproduced or transmitted in any form or by any means, electronic or mechanical, including photocopying, recording or by any information storage and retrieval system, without the written permission of the publisher.

Limit of Liability/Disclaimer of Warranty: While the publisher and sailor have used their best efforts not to offend while preparing this book, some people will no doubt be offended. As a result, no representations or warranties are made or inferred with respect to the accuracy or completeness of this book, or the truth of any of the statements. It comes with no warranties, implied or otherwise, of merchantability or fitness for a particular purpose. We do not guarantee that any of the people mentioned in this book are real, and if they are real, no similarity is intended or inferred. Should the people in this book actually exist, this book makes no character sailorment about them or their friends, families, relatives and other people they may know now, in the future or in the past. Be warned. The jokes in this book may not suit your needs or tastes. If you are concerned about being offended, and have already paid for this book, put it down now and take steps to destroy it, as neither the publisher or sailor shall be liable for any damages or losses made to any groups of people or individuals who may or may not be mentioned in this book. This includes, but is not limited to special, incidental, consequential or other damages. YOU HAVE BEEN WARNED.

Dolyttle & Seamore
198 Garth Road Suite 2DD
Scarsdale, NY 10583

Publisher's Cataloging-in-Publication Data

The Best Ever Book of Jokes: Lots and Lots of Jokes Specially Repurposed for Sailors.

p. cm.
ISBN-13:1468114298
ISBN-10:9781468114294

10 9 8 7 6 5 4 3 2 1

To All Those People
Who Think They Have a Sense of Humor —But Don't

Introduction

In my world, nothing is original. While I may be the only person who believes this, it's true. I have heard almost every joke in this book at least a hundred times—the only difference is the victim—a different ethnic, racial or religious group.

I grew up in Australia where the victim was Irish. In other states and countries the victim is often Jewish, Blond, Italian, Libyan, Catholic, Mexican, Polish, Australian, Norwegian, Essex Girl, Newfie, Mother-in-Law, etc.

Just because the person being picked on varies from country to country, it doesn't mean they're a hated minority. I would argue that it means that they're loved (after all, almost everybody wants to be the center of attention). In most cases, the goal is not humiliation, because the jokes being told are not nasty—they're funny—or at least they're supposed to be.

With that said, sit down, put on your happy face and prepare to be transported back to a time when you were young and innocent, and your friends tried to put a smile on your face.

And, if you're offended, sorry, no offence is intended. Just remember that perception is everything, and the way you perceive these jokes says a lot about you.

Mark Young

Why do people take an instant dislike to sailors?

To save time later.

Two sailors were helping a friend open a new store, and decided to take a break. Since the shop wasn't due to open for a few days, the shelves were not fully set up.

One sailor said to the other: "I bet some old fogey will walk by, put his or her face to the window, and ask what we're selling."

No sooner were the words out of his mouth, when an old woman peeked through the window and cheerfully asked: "What are you selling?"

"We're selling assholes," replied one of the sailors sarcastically.

Without skipping a beat, the lovely old lady said: "You must be doing well. You've only got two left."

What do you call a sailor who practices birth control??

A humanitarian.

Why do sailors make great astronauts?

They took up space in school.

Two sailors were riding their bikes across a university campus when one said: "Where did you get such a great bike?"

The second sailor said: "I was walking across town yesterday, minding my own business, when a beautiful woman rode up on this bike, threw it to the ground, took off all her clothes and said: "Take what you want.""

The first sailor nodded approvingly and said: "Good choice; the clothes probably wouldn't have fit you anyway."

There was a sailor who was late for work during the power failure because he got stuck on the escalator.

Two sailors in a kayak were chilly, so they lit a fire in the craft. It sank, proving once again that you can't have your kayak and heat it too.

A sailor was staying with a friend and asked if there was anything he could do to help out.

"Sure," said the friend. "I'd really appreciate it if you could pick up a carton of milk when you're out. If they have eggs, get six."

A couple of hours later the sailor returned with six cartons of milk.

"Why did you buy six cartons of milk?," asked the friend.

"They had eggs," replied the sailor.

Why did the sailor cut a hole in the carpet?

To see a floor show.

Did you hear about the sailor who went to a mind reader?

There was no charge.

Why don't sailors eat pickles?

They can't get their head in the jar.

A sailor met a fairy who said she would grant her one wish.

"I want to live forever," said the sailor.

"Sorry," said the fairy. "I can't grant wishes like that!"

"Fine," said the sailor. "I want to live until Congress gets its heads out of its ass!"

"Crafty bastard," said the fairy.

A sailor with one ear want into a bar.

"Do you want a beer?," asked the sailor.

The sailor: "I've got one ear."

Four workers were on the top floor of a high-rise building project when Steve fell off the roof and died instantly.

After the body was taken away by the ambulance, they held a meeting to decide who would tell Steve's wife that he was killed in a horrible accident.

Finally, one of the workers said: "I used to be a sailor, so I'm pretty good at delivering bad news, I'll do it."

Two hours later, he came back carrying a case of beer.

"Where did you get the beer?," asked one of the workers.

"Steve's wife gave it to me," he said.

The worker replies: "That's unbelievable, you told the lady her husband was dead and she gave you the beer?"

"Well not exactly," said the sailor. "When Steve's wife answered the door, I said to her: 'You must be Steve's widow.'"

She said: "No, I'm not a widow."

And I said: "I'll bet you a case of beer you are."

How did the sailor die ice fishing?

She was run over by the Zamboni machine.

Hear about the sailor who broke both legs ironing the curtains?

She fell out the window.

An evil genie captured a sailor and her two friends and banished them to the desert for a week. The genie allowed each person to bring one thing.

The first friend brought a canteen so he wouldn't die of thirst.

The second friend brought an umbrella to keep the sun off.

The sailor brought a car door, because if it got too hot she could just roll down the window!

Did you hear about the sailor who broke an arm raking leaves?

Fell out of the tree"

A sailor took a second job in a restaurant to earn some extra cash for the holidays. All went well until the boss said: "Please fill the salt shakers."

It took the sailor three hours to put the salt through the hole in the top of the container.

Three sailors took a small plane to the wilderness in northern Canada to hunt moose over a weekend. The pilot said: "Please remember that this is a very small plane. You can only bring back one moose between you."

But of course each sailor killed their own moose and come Sunday, they told the pilot that last year

they each brought their own moose on the plane. The pilot agreed to let them take all three dead moose home.

Just after takeoff, the plane stalled and crashed. In the wreckage, one of the sailors woke up, looked around and said: "Where the hell are we."

"Oh, about a hundred yards east of the place where we crashed last year," replied one of the other sailors.

Did you hear about the sailor who lost $50 on a baseball game?

He lost another $50 on the replay.

What do you call a sailor on a Harley wearing a leather jacket?

A rebel without a clue.

A crooked sailor and two other prisoners escaped from jail. They ran into the woods and all hid in the trees.

When the guard shined his flashlight up the tree, the first prisoner said "meow." The guard said: "It's just a cat."

When the guard shined his flashlight up the next tree, the prisoner said: "whooo, whooo." The guard said: "It's just an owl."

When he shined his flashlight up the third tree, the sailor said: "Moo, moo."

How many sailor jokes are there?

None, they're all facts.

A sailor was asked to be the Groomsman at a friend's wedding, but had to refuse because he didn't know anything about horses.

A sailor was being honored by his peers at an award dinner, when suddenly there was a flash of light and God appeared before the sailor.

God, turned to the sailor and said: "You have made a great contribution to your field and I would like to reward you for everything you've done. You have the choice of infinite wealth, boundless wisdom or utter beauty. Pick one."

Without hesitating, the sailor said: "Wisdom."

"Done!," said God, and disappeared in a cloud of smoke and a bolt of lightning.

There was a great silence as everyone looked at the sailor. Finally, a voice called out: "Say something wise."

The sailor turned to the crowd and said: "I should have taken the money."

There was a sailor who sent 10 puns to friends, hoping that at least one of the puns would make them laugh. No pun in ten did.

How do you make a sailor laugh on Monday morning?

Tell her a joke on Friday night.

Three sailors driving from Boston to Disneyland.

After three days they arrived at their destination and turned around and went home after they saw the sign saying: "Disneyland left."

A sailor was taken to the hospital after suffering a heart attack. While on the operating table, the sailor had a near death experience. Seeing God, she asked: "Is my time up?"

God said: "No, you have another 15 years, 2 months and 8 days to live."

Upon recovery, the sailor decided to get a face lift, liposuction and a tummy tuck.

Upon release from hospital, the sailor crossed the street, was killed by a bus.

Arriving in heaven the sailor screamed at God: "You said I had another 15 years? Why didn't you pull me from out of the bus's path?"

God replied: "I'm sorry, I didn't recognize you."

A sailor was driving down I-95 when her cell phone rang. Her friend said: "Be careful, there's a car going the wrong way on I-95."

The sailor replied: "They got it wrong, it's not one car, it's hundreds of them!"

Do you know how to save a drowning sailor?

No?... Good!

A sailor was walking down the street with a brown paper bag. He ran into one of his friends who asked what was in the bag. The sailor said: "Fish."

The friend said if I can guess how many fish you have in the bag, you'll have to give me one."

The sailor said: "I'll tell you what, if you can tell me how many fish I have, I'll give you both of them."

Why won't a shark attack a sailor swimming in the ocean?

Professional courtesy.

A sailor received a parrot as a gift. The parrot had a bad attitude and an even worse vocabulary. Every word out of the bird's mouth was rude, obnoxious and laced with profanity.

The sailor tried to change the bird's attitude by saying only polite words, playing soft music and doing anything possible to "clean up" the bird's vocabulary.

Finally, the sailor was fed up and yelled at the
parrot. The parrot yelled back. The sailor shook the parrot, and the parrot got angrier and angrier and ruder and ruder. In desperation, the sailor grabbed the bird and put him in the freezer.

For a few minutes the parrot squawked and kicked and screamed. Then suddenly there was total quiet. Not a peep was heard for over a minute. Fearing that he'd hurt the parrot, the sailor opened the door to the freezer.

The parrot calmly stepped out into the sailor's arms and said: "I believe I may have offended you with my rude language and actions. I'm sincerely remorseful for my inappropriate transgressions and I fully intend to do everything I can to correct my rude and unforgivable behavior."

The sailor was stunned at the change in the bird's attitude.

As the sailor was about to ask the parrot why he had made such a dramatic change in his behavior, the bird spoke-up, very softly and said: "May I ask what the turkey did?"

Where can you find a good sailor?

In the cemetery.

Did you hear about the sailor who froze to death outside a theater?

He was waiting to see the movie "Closed for the Winter."

A sailor went out bear hunting and spotted one in the bushes and blasted away. The sailor investigated but couldn't find the bear. As he was about to give up, he felt tap tap on his shoulder and when he turned around
saw the bear.

The bear said: "You know, it's not bear hunting season?"

The sailor answered: "Yes, I know."

The bear took the rifle and smashed it on a rock, threw the hunter across a tree trunk, pulls his pants down and gave it to him. He then told the sailor: "Get out of here. I don't want to see you again."

The sailor was incensed, so he raced back to town and bought the biggest bear rifle he could find, and returned to the forest. A few minutes later, he spotted the bear and emptied his rifle. He then searched for the body, but couldn't
find it.

He then felt a tap on his shoulder, and surprise, surprise, it was the bear again.

"I thought I told you not to come back," said the bear. The bear then proceeded to smash the new rifle, and again threw the sailor to the ground and gave it to him again. "This is the last time I'm warning you. Don't come back."

The sailor went berserk. When he got back to
town, he bought a M16 and went straight back to the forest.
Thinking he saw the bear in a bush, he took aim and emptied
the entire M16. Still no body, until, a familiar tap on the
shoulder.

"You're not in this for the hunting, are you?," asks the bear.

Friend: "Please close the window. It's cold outside."

Sailor: "If I close the window, will it get warm outside?"

Why did the sailor die while drinking milk?

The cow fell on her.

A sailor was worried that his wife was losing her hearing and
he thought she might need a hearing aid. Not
quite sure what to do, he called the family doctor to discuss
the problem.

The doctor suggested a simple informal test that he could
perform to test his wife's hearing loss. "Stand about 40 feet
away from your wife," said the doctor, "and in a normal
speaking voice ask her a question. If she doesn't respond, go to
30 feet, then 20 feet, and so on until you get a response."

That evening, the sailor's wife was in the kitchen cooking dinner, and he was watching TV in the family room. He says to himself: "I'm about 40 feet away, let's see what happens."

In a normal tone he asks: 'Honey, what's for dinner?" No response. So the sailor moved closer to the kitchen, about 30 feet from his wife and repeated the question.
Still no response.

He then went into the dining room, where he was about 20 feet from his wife and asked the question a third time. Again no response.

He then walked up to the kitchen door, about 10 feet away from his wife and loudly repeated the question. Still nothing.

Finally he walks up to her and calmly says: "Honey, what's for dinner?"

"For the fifth time, we're having spaghetti," said the wife.

How do you sink a sailor's submarine?

Knock on the hatch.

A sailor from Montreal sent his photo to a lonely hearts club.

They wrote back saying they weren't that lonely.

A sailor is at the post office buying stamps for her holiday cards.

"May I have 50 Chanukah stamps and 50 Christmas stamps?, said the sailor."

The clerk asked: "What denomination?"

"Oh my god!," the woman exclaimed. "Has it really come to this? Give me 16 Orthodox, 22 Conservative and 12 Reform Chanukah cards, and 20 Catholic, 18 Greek Orthodox and 12 Lutheran Christmas stamps."

A sailor was refused service in a restaurant. "We don't serve sailors here," said the waiter.

That's OK said the sailor, I don't eat sailors."

How can you confuse a sailor?

You can't. They're born that way.

After being married for 44 years, a sailor took a careful look at his wife one day and said: "Darling, 44 years ago we had a cheap apartment, a junky car, slept on a sofa bed and watched a 10-inch black and white TV. But I got to sleep with a hot 21-year-old girl every night. Now I have a million dollar home, a $60,000 car, a big bed and a large-screen TV, but I'm living with a 65-year-old woman. It seems to me that you're not holding up your side of things."

The sailor's wife replied: "No problem. If that's what you want, go for it. If you want to sleep with a 21-year-old, I'll make sure you once again get to live a cheap apartment, drive a junky car, sleep on a sofa bed and watch a 10-inch black-and-white TV!"

Did you hear about the man who wanted to be buried at sea?

His sailor died trying to dig the grave

Why did the sailor write TGIF on his shoes?

To remind him that Toes Go In First.

If you see a sailor on a bicycle, why shouldn't you hit him?

He might be riding your bicycle.

A sailor and his wife were sitting around the breakfast table one lazy Sunday morning. The sailor turned to his wife and said: "When I die, I want you to sell all my stuff."

"Why would you want me to do that?," asked his wife.

"I figure that you'll eventually remarry, and I don't want some asshole using my stuff," replied the sailor.

The sailor's spouse said: "What makes you think I'd marry another asshole?"

A police officer pulled over a sailor and asked to see his license.

The sailor said: "I wish you would make up your mind. Yesterday when you pulled me over you took away my license—now you want me to show it to you."

Why did God make snakes just before sailors?

Practice.

A sailor walked into a bar with his alligator and asked the sailor if they served sailors.

"Sure do," replied the sailor.

"Great," said the sailor. "Give me a beer, and I'll have a sailor for my alligator."

There was a sailor flying in a helicopter to a town 50 miles away. Suddenly everything went black.

After they crashed the pilot said: "What happened?"

The sailor said: "I got cold, so I turned off the fan."

Ship's captain: "Please divert your course 15 degrees to the north to avoid a collision."

Sailor: "Recommend you divert your course 15 degrees to the south to avoid a collision."

Ship's captain: "This is the captain of a US Navy ship. I say again, divert your course."

Sailor: "No. I say again, you divert your course."

Ship's captain: "This is the aircraft carrier USS Lincoln, the second largest ship in the United States Atlantic fleet. We are accompanied by three destroyers, three cruisers and numerous support vessels. I demand that you change your course 15 degrees north. That's one-five degrees north, or counter measures will be undertaken to ensure the safety of this ship."

Sailor: "I'm a sailor on vacation with my family in a lighthouse. Your call."

What's the difference between a sailor and a bucket of dirt?

The bucket.

A sailor and a friend were sitting in a bar, drinking beer.

The sailor turned to his friend and said: "I'm tired of going through life being a drain on society. Tomorrow, I'm going to go down to the college and enroll in a class that will help me make society a better place."

The next day, the sailor goes down to the college, meets the admissions officer and enrolls in a course called Logic.

At the first class, the lecturer explains that logic helps you to figure out how the world works. To demonstrate, he calls the sailor up to the front of the classroom.

The lecturer asks: "Do you own a weed eater?"

"Yes," replies the sailor.

"Then logically speaking, I could reasonably conclude that you have a yard," said the lecturer.

"True," said the sailor, "I do have a yard."

The lecturer went on. "Because you have a yard, I think that you also have a house."

"That's right," said the sailor.

"And, because you have a house, there's also a good chance that you have a family."

"Right again," said the sailor. "I do have a family."

"I'm not done," said the lecturer. "Because you have a family, then logically you must have a wife. And, because you have a wife, logic tells me you must be a heterosexual."

"I am a heterosexual," replied the sailor. "I'm impressed that you were able to work out so much about me without me having to say a word—just because I own a weed eater."

A couple of weeks later, the sailor and his friend are again drinking. He tells his friend that he's studying logic, and offers to demonstrate his new-found knowledge.

The sailor asks his friend: "Do you own a weed eater?"

"No," replied the friend.

"Then you're gay," proclaimed the sailor.

Did you hear about the terrorists who hijacked a plane full of sailors?

They threatened to release one each hour until their demands were met.

There was a sailor who waited two hours at the side door of a movie theatre to see the stars come out.

A sailor was watching the scuba divers jump off a boat when his friend turned to him and said: "Why do the scuba divers always fall backwards off the boats?"

The sailor replied: "Because if they fell forwards they'd still be in the boat, wouldn't they?"

Four sailors were on a plane to Las Vegas for a conference when the first sailor said: "We've all worked together for many years, but don't really know one another. I suggest we tell each other something about ourselves that nobody knows.

They look nervously at each other, but nod OK. The first sailor says: "Since I suggested it, I'll go first. With me it's alcohol. Every so often, I go down to a bar and drink myself silly for a few days. Not only can't I remember what I did, I have to make up an excuse to explain my absence."

They all look each other nervously, but the next sailor slowly starts: "With me, it's gambling. Periodically,

I go down to the casino and spend a couple of months salary, and then have to explain to my wife what happened. Not easy."

The third sailor, who is really nervous, reluctantly says: "This is very difficult. With me it's women. Every so often I go down to the red light district, pick out a girl, and spend a week in the saddle. I really have problems explaining where I've been to my wife."

They all look at the fourth sailor, waiting. He doesn't say anything. Then one of the four speaks up: "Come now, we've all told our innermost faults. It's your turn."

He looks at the others and starts hesitantly.

"Well," he says, "I'm an inveterate gossip, and I can't wait to get off this plane."

How do you confuse a sailor?

Place three shovels against a wall and ask him to take his pick.

What is the difference between a sailor and a pothole?

People don't run over the same pothole more than once.

A couple recently celebrated their 50th wedding anniversary and invited their three sons, all very successful sailors, to a dinner that was being hosted by their local community to celebrate this momentous occasion.

The first son arrived 30 minutes late and said: "Happy anniversary. Sorry I'm late, but there was a lot of traffic on the freeway and I didn't have time to get you a gift."

"Not to worry," said the father. "The important thing is that we're together today."

Son number two arrived 45 minutes late and announced: "Happy anniversary. You and mom look great. I had a last minute meeting with a client, and I only just made my plane. Sorry, but I didn't have time to shop for you."

"Don't even think about it," said the father, "we're glad you were able to come."

Five minutes later their youngest son arrived from across town and said: "Hello and happy anniversary! I'm sorry, but my boss made me work today and I was so busy packing for my vacation, I didn't have time to get you anything."

"It's fine," said the father, "at least we're all here."

After they had finished dessert, and the members of the community had dispersed, the father turned to his three sailor children and said: "There's something your mother and I have wanted to tell you for a long time.

"When we were young, we were very poor. Despite this, we were able to send each of you to college. Throughout the years your mother and I knew that we loved each other very much, but we just never found the time to get married."

The three children gasped and son number two said: "You mean we're all bastards?"

"Yes," said the father.

"And cheap ones too."

Why did the sailor cut a hole in his umbrella?

So he could see when it stopped raining.

Why don't they give sailors coffee breaks?

It takes too long to retrain them.

Two sailors went out one night and got very drunk. Thinking it wasn't a good idea to drive, they decided to walk. After a few minutes, one sailor said: "I'm tired and drunk, I'm never going to make it home."

Since they had no money for a cab, they kept walking until they hit the bus terminal. The two sailors looked at each other and one said: "Why don't we steal a bus?"

"Good idea," said the other.

One sailor stood guard, and the other went inside to steal a bus. After 15 minutes, the sailor yells: "What's happening? Haven't you found a bus yet."

The other sailor screams back: "I can't find a 52."

"No problem," replies the other. "Just grab a 75 and we'll walk from the traffic lights."

A sailor was telling his friend why his rent had gone up. "I told the landlord that I wanted to live in a more expensive apartment, so he raised my rent."

Why do sailors wear slip-on shoes?

You need an IQ of at least 4 to tie a shoelace.

A sailor was lost wandering around the desert when he came across a clothing store. Desperate for a drink, he went inside and asked the owner if he could have a glass of water.

"I'm sorry," said the store owner, "you're in the middle of the desert, I don't have any water —but I could sell you a nice tie."

"I don't need a tie," screamed the sailor. "I need a glass of water."

Maintaining his composure, the storeowner said: "I'm sorry that I don't have any water, but over that big hill is a restaurant where you'll be able to buy food, water or any type of drink you want."

The sailor left cursing and started walking toward the hill.

An hour later, the totally dehydrated sailor returned. "I'd like to buy a tie please," he said.

"What made you change your mind," asked the storeowner.

"Your brother wouldn't let me into his restaurant without a tie."

A sailor goes to his doctor and asks for the result of the tests.

"I have bad news and worse news," says the doctor.

"Oh dear, what's the bad news?," asks the sailor.

The doctor replies: "You only have 24 hours to live."

"That's terrible," said the sailor. "How could the news possibly get any worse?"

The doctor replies: "I've been trying to call you since yesterday!"

What's the difference between a sailor and a gigolo?

A gigolo only screws one person at a time.

A short balding sailor is sitting at the bar staring at his drink when a large, trouble-making biker steps up next to him, grabs his drink and gulps it down in one swig.

"Whatcha gonna do about it?," asks the biker menacingly, as the sailor bursts into tears.

"Come on," says the biker. "I didn't think you'd cry. I can't stand to see a man crying."

"This is the worst day of my life," said the sailor.

"I'm a complete failure. I was late to a meeting and my boss fired me. Then I went to the parking lot and discovered that my car had been stolen and that my insurance had expired. I hailed a cab, forgot my wallet on the back seat and went home. When I got there, I found my wife in bed with another guy and my dog attacked me.

"Feeling depressed, I came to this bar to work up the courage to end it all. I bought a drink, dropped the suicide capsule in it, and sat here trying to get the nerve to swallow it, when you showed up and grabbed the drink out of my hands.

"I can't even commit suicide. It's just not my day."

A sailor walks into the bakery and buys a cherry pie.

"Would you like it cut into four pieces or eight pieces?," asked the salesgirl.

"Better make that four pieces," said the sailor. "I'm on a diet."

A waiter comes over to a table full of sailors and asks, "Is anything all right?

A sailor owned a small ranch in Montana. The Montana Department of Labor claimed he wasn't paying his employees properly and sent an agent out to interview him.

"I need a list of your employees and the documentation showing how much you pay them," demanded the agent.

"No problem," replied the sailor. "I have a farm hand who's been with me for three years. He earns $700 a week for 40 hours, plus free room and board.

"Then there's the cook. She's worked for me for 18 months. I pay her $550 per week for 40 hours, plus free room and board.

"Then there's the half-wit," said the sailor. "He works at least 18 hours every day, and does 90% of the work. He makes around $50 per week and pays for his own room and board.

When times are good, he gets a free bottle of bourbon on Saturday night.

"I want to meet the half-wit," says the agent.

"Pleased to make your acquaintance," replied the sailor.

What's a definition of disappointment?

A busload of sailors going off the edge of a cliff—with one empty seat.

One winter morning a sailor and her husband were listening to the radio during breakfast.

The announcer came on and said: "We're expecting 8- to 10-inches of snow today. Park your car on the even-numbered side of the street, so the snowplows can get through."

Not wanting to get a ticket, the sailor went outside and moved the car to the even-numbered side of the road.

A week later, the announcer said: "It's a miserable winter. We're expecting another 10- to 12-inches of snow today. Park your car on the odd-numbered side of the street, so the snowplows can get through."

The sailor went out and moved her car to the odd-numbered side of the street.

The same thing happened a couple of days later when they were having breakfast, but before they could hear which side of the street to park the car, the power went out.

"What do we do now?," said the sailor. "I have no idea where to park the car."

The husband said: "Why don't you just leave it in the garage?"

A sailor was drinking with a few friends. After the bar closed, a drunk sailor brought a few of his friends back to his new apartment so they could keep the party going for a couple of hours.

He took them into the living room where there was a big brass gong and a mallet.

"What's that brass gong?," one of the guests asked.

"It's not a gong, it's a talking clock," the sailor replied.

"No way," replied his astonished friend.

"Yup," replied the drunk sailor.

"How's it work?," the friend asked.

"Watch," the drunk sailor replied. He picked up the mallet, gave it an ear-shattering pound and stepped back.

The three friends stood looking at one another, when all of a sudden someone on the other side of the wall screamed: "You asshole! It's 3:15 in the morning!"

What do you call a sailor with half a brain?

Gifted.

An elderly sailor and his wife were having dinner at another couple's house. After eating, the wives left the table and went into the kitchen to get some coffee for the men.

The two gentlemen were talking, and the sailor said: "Last night we went to a new restaurant and it was really great. I recommend it very highly."

The other man said: "What's the name of the restaurant?"

The sailor thought and thought and finally said: "What is the name of the flower you give to someone you love? You know, it's red and has thorns."

"You mean a rose?," asked the friend

"Yes," said the sailor. He then yelled: "Rose, what's the name of the restaurant we went to last night?"

Why did the sailor climb over the glass wall?

To see what was on the other side.

During a recent password audit, it was found that a sailor was using the following password:

MickeyMinniePlutoHueyLouieDeweyDonaldGoofySacramento

When they asked the sailor why she needed such a long password, she said she was told that it had to be eight characters long and include at least one capital.

How do you keep a sailor busy for hours?

Write "please turn over" on both sides of a piece of paper.

How do you drive a sailor crazy?

Give him a bag of M&Ms and tell him to alphabetize them.

A sailor was walking to the deli along with two of his employees when he tripped over a bottle.

The sailor picked the bottle up, rubbed the sides and a genie appeared. The genie offered each of them one wish.

"I wish I was on a beach in a tropical island," said the first employee. Immediately her wish was granted.

"I wish I was on a tour of France," said the second employee. Immediately his wish too, was granted.

It was now time for the sailor to make his wish.

"I want my employees back in their offices right after lunch," moaned the sailor.

What do sailors use for birth control?

Their personalities.

A circus owner ran an ad for a lion tamer and two people showed up. One was a sailor and the other a blonde in her mid-twenties.

The circus owner tells them: "I'm not going to sugar coat it. This is one ferocious lion. He ate my last tamer so you guys better be good or you're history. Here's your equipment—a chair, whip and a gun. Who wants to try out first?"

The girl says: "I'll go first." She walks right past the chair, the whip and the gun and steps right into the lion's cage. The lion starts to snarl and pant and begins to charge her. About half way there, she throws open her coat revealing her beautiful naked body. The lion stops dead in his tracks, sheepishly crawls up to her and starts licking her feet and ankles. He continues to lick and kiss her entire body for several minutes and then rests his head on her feet.

The circus owner's mouth is on the floor. He says: "I've never seen a display like that in my life." He then turns to the sailor and asks: "Can you top that?"

The sailor replies: "No problem, just get that lion out of the way."

A sailor was sitting in a bar having a drink and watching the 10 o'clock news. There was a story about a man on a ledge of a building preparing to jump came on. The sailor turns to the customer next to him asked: "Do you think he'll jump?"

The customer says: "I bet he'll jump."

The sailor says: "I bet you $20 he won't."

Just as the customer placed her money on the bar, the guy jumped off of the building, falling to his death.

The sailor handed his $20 to the customer and said: "All's fair. Here's your money."

The customer replies: "I can't take your money. I saw the 6 o'clock news and knew he'd jump."

"So did I," said the sailor, "but I didn't think he'd do it again."

Did you hear about the sailor who locked his keys in his car?

He needed a coat hanger to get his family out.

Three friends went down to Mexico one night, got drunk, and woke up in jail, only to find that they were to be executed in the morning. Unfortunately, none of them could remember what they did the night before.

The first friend was strapped in the electric chair, and was asked if she had any last words.

She said: "I believe in the almighty power of God to intervene on the behalf of the innocent." The prison warden threw the switch and nothing happened.

Immediately, the prison warden begs her for forgiveness, and sets her free.

The second friend is strapped in and says: "I am a law student and I believe in the power of justice to intervene on the part of the innocent." They threw the switch again, nothing happened.

The prison warden begs her for forgiveness, and releases her.

The last one, a sailor, is strapped in and says: "Before I became a sailor, I was an electrician, and I can tell you right now, you're not going to electrocute anybody if you don't plug this thing in."

A sailor was on a United flight to Australia and the flight attendant asked him if he wanted any dinner.

"What are my choices?," asked the sailor.

"Yes or no," replied the flight attendant.

What's the difference between a sailor and a vulture?

Vultures wait until you're dead to rip your heart out.

The sailor was sitting in a fine restaurant with his wife when she looked over at a nearby table and saw a man in a drunken stupor.

The sailor said: "You've been watching that man for some time now. Do you know him?"

"Yes," replied the wife. "He's my ex-husband. He's been drinking like that since I left him seven years ago."

"That's amazing," the sailor replies, "I didn't think anybody could celebrate for that long."

Did you hear about the lion walking through the woods eating deer droppings?

He had just eaten a sailor and was trying to get the taste out of his mouth!

A sailor walked into a bar and ordered martini after martini, each time removing the olives and placing them in a jar.

When the jar was filled with olives, the sailor got up to leave.

"Excuse me," said a customer, who was puzzled over what the sailor had done. "Why did you put all the olives from your drinks in the jar?"

The sailor replied: "My wife just sent me out for a jar of olives!"

What do sailors and sperm have in common?

A sperm has one-in-3 million chance of actually becoming a human being.

Three friends were stumbling home from a bar one night and found themselves on the road which led past the old cemetery.

"Come have a look over here," said one friend. "It's Michael Rosenbaum's grave. He lived to the ripe old age of 87."

"That's nothing," said the second friend. "Here's one named Patrick Bradley, it says here that he was 95 when he died."

Just then, the sailor yells out: "Good God, here's a guy who lived to be 145!"

"What was his name?," asks friend number two.

The sailor stumbles, and awkwardly lights a match to see what else is written on the stone marker, and exclaims: "It's Miles, from Dallas."

How do you get a sailor to laugh at a joke on Saturday?

Tell it to him on Wednesday.

A sailor needed a vacation and decided that ice fishing was what he needed to relieve his tension.

After arriving at his destination a couple of days later, he started to drill, when all of a sudden he heard a loud booming voice yelling: "There's no fish down there."

He stopped, moved over a few feet and started drilling for a second time. Again, he heard the loud booming voice yelling: "There's no fish down there."

So the sailor moved over about 50 feet and started to drill for the third time. The same loud booming voice again broke the silence and said: "There's no fish there either."

Getting nervous, the sailor looked around, saw nobody and asked: "Who are you? God?"

"No," replied the booming voice. "I'm the ice skating arena manager."

What do you call 25 skydiving sailors?

Skeet.

A sailor and his friend were both patients in a mental hospital. One day, while they were walking around the hospital's swimming pool, his friend jumped into the pool and promptly sank to the bottom.

Thinking quickly, the sailor jumped in and pulled his friend out.

When the medical director heard about the sailor's heroic act, he immediately ordered him released as he was considered mentally stable.

When he went to tell the sailor the news he said: "I have good news and bad news. The good news is you're being discharged, as you were able to rationally respond to a crisis by jumping in and saving your friend's life.

"The bad news is that your friend hung himself in the bathroom with his bathrobe belt right after you saved him."

The sailor said: "He didn't hang himself, I hung him there to dry. How soon can I go home?"

What's the difference between a dead skunk on the road and a dead sailor on the road?

Vultures will eat the skunk.

A sailor walks into a bar. The bartender asks: "What will you have?"

The sailor says: "Give me three pints of beer, please."

So the bartender brings him three pints and the man proceeds to alternately sip one, then the other, then the third until they're gone. He then orders three more.

The bartender says: "I know you like them cold. You don't have to order three at a time. I can keep an eye on it, and when you're low, bring you a fresh cold one."

"You don't understand," said the sailor. "I have two brothers, one in Dallas and one in Nevada. We made a vow to each other that every Saturday night we'd still drink together. So right now, each of my brothers has three beers, and we're drinking together."

The bartender thought that was a wonderful tradition.

Every week the man came in and ordered three beers. Then one week he came in and ordered only two. He drank them and then ordered two more.

"I know your tradition," said the bartender. "And I'd just like to let you know that I'm sorry one of your brothers died."

"My brothers are fine," said the sailor. "I only ordered two beers because I've quit drinking."

———

A sailor was working on a construction site to earn extra cash. The boss needed a wheelbarrow. A short time later the sailor returned with two wheelbarrows, one on top of another.

The boss said: "I only wanted one."

The sailor said: "What did you want me to do, carry it?"

———

A sailor was flying to New York in a four-engine plane, when the pilot announced that one engine had failed and there would be a 30-minute delay. The pilot said there was no reason for concern as the jet had three more engines. The same announcement was made two more times.

Finally, the sailor turned to the person in the next seat and said: "I hope the other engine doesn't fail, or we'll be up here all day."

What's the difference between a sailor and a trampoline?

You take off your shoes before you jump on a trampoline.

A sailor was touring Europe in a chauffeur-driven Mercedes-Benz. The sailor asked the driver what the emblem on the front of the car was for.

The driver said it was to line up parking inspectors. Nothing else was said until they saw a parking inspector writing tickets.

The sailor asked the driver to demonstrate the device. The driver carefully lined up the parking inspector and went straight for him—swerving at the last minute.

Suddenly there was a loud bang. "What happened?," asked the driver.

"The sailor said: "You would have missed him if I hadn't opened the door."

An elderly sailor is hit by a car and brought to the hospital.

The nurse asks: "Are you comfortable, sir?"

The sailor replied: "I make a living."

A sailor hired a plumber to do a couple of jobs around his house. When he received the bill he was angry to find he had been charged $350 an hour.

The sailor said: "I'm a sailor and I don't earn that much.

The plumber said: "Neither did I when I was a sailor. "

Did you hear the sad story about the sailor who was given a pill that was supposed to radically increase a person's IQ. When it was given to rats, they were able to run a maze with one eye closed in half the time it took the other rats to complete the course.

Needless to say, the doctors were anxious to try it out on humans. When approval was granted, they gave it to several people including a sailor, who took it faithfully every day.

Two years later, the sailor earned a degree in brain surgery—an all time record.

Unfortunately, the sailor was part of the control group that had been given a placebo. There he was, dumb as ever, and stuck with an advanced medical degree. What a waste. Really sad.

A sailor was sitting at a bar when he notices a lamp on the bookshelf. He wanders over and begins to rub it.

Out pops a genie and offers him three wishes. Immediately he says I want a glass of beer that automatically refills itself.

A glass of beer appears. The sailor drinks it quickly, and it immediately refills itself. He does the same thing two more times.

The genie then asks what he wants for his other two wishes.

Without thinking, the sailor says quickly: "I'll take another two of these."

Two sailors were driving to their new jobs in Florida, when they saw a sign which said "Clean bathrooms."

By the time they had reached Florida, they had cleaned 32 bathrooms.

A sailor and another person applied for a part-time job waitressing to earn some extra money. Being a high-class

establishment, the owner of the bar gave them both a 10 question test to determine who should get the job.

Both applicants handed in the test, and they both correctly answered the first nine questions.

The bar owner then went up to the sailor and said: "You both got question 10 wrong, but based on the way you answered the question, I've decided to hire the other person.

"What do you mean?," said the sailor. "How could one wrong answer be better than another wrong answer?"

"Simple," replied the bar owner. "On question 10, the other applicant wrote: 'I don't know,' and you wrote 'neither do I.'"

What is the first thing you should do if you find a sailor buried up to his neck in cement?

Get more cement.

A young, sailor was walking around a field in Long Island, when he came across an old lamp. He rubbed the lamp and suddenly a genie appeared before him.

"For freeing me, I will grant you one wish," said the genie.

"I wish that there was a bridge from New York to London so I don't get ripped off every time I go on vacation," said the sailor.

"I'm sorry, but I can't do that," said the genie. "It would be too much change. Thousands of people would be put out of work.

Government revenue would be reduced dramatically. It would mess up too many people's lives."

So the sailor thought for a second and said: "OK, then. I'm a sailor, and I'm tired of everyone making fun of me. I wish that sailors were as smart, or smarter than everyone else in the world."

The genie said: "Would you like two lanes, or four?"

Three sailors were waiting to be interviewed for a job. The first sailor was called into the office, and after the normal questions was told that he would have to answer a question that tested his verbal skills.

The interviewer said: "I would like you to make a sentence using the word 'sweater.'"

The sailor said: "My mother knitted me a sweater."

"I'll get back to you," said the interviewer. "Please ask the next applicant to come in."

After the second sailor's interview he also was asked make a sentence using the word "sweater."

The second sailor said: "My mother knitted me a sweater."

Of course, the interviewer was suspicious, but he told the sailor that he would get back to him.

Getting wise, the interviewer changed the question for the third sailor. Instead of asking him to use the word "sweater," he asked him to use "fascinate."

The sailor said: "My mother knitted me a nice sweater with 10 buttons, but I can only fasten eight."

How can you tell if a sailor is lying?

His lips are moving.

A sailor returned home one night when he came across a dead body on his lawn. Thinking quickly, he called 911 and reported the incident.

"Where's the body," asked the 911 operator.

"It's at the end of Eucalyptus Drive," the sailor replied.

"Could you please spell that for me?," the operator asked.

After a long pause, the sailor said: "How about if I drag the body over to Oak Street and you pick it up there?"

What's the difference between a sailor and a vampire?

A vampire only sucks blood at night.

A sailor was walking down the street with a case of beer under his arm when his friend Peter stopped him and asked what he got the case of beer for.

"I got it for my partner," replied the sailor.

"Good trade," replied Peter.

A sailor and two of his friends walked into a bar and ordered three beers.

Just as they were about to take a drink, three flies appeared and jumped into each glass.

The first friend pushed away the beer in disgust. The second friend scooped the fly out of the beer and started drinking as if nothing had happened.

The sailor picked the fly out of his drink and started shaking it over his drink and began yelling: "Spit it out. Come on already, spit it out."

What's black and brown and looks good on an account sailor?

A Doberman pinscher.

What's the difference between a dead skunk on the road and a dead sailor on the road?

Skid marks in front of the skunk.

You are in a room with a mass murderer, a terrorist and a sailor.

You have a gun with only two bullets.

What do you do?

Shoot the sailor twice.

A sailor dies and goes to hell. The devil greets him warmly at the gates, and as they enter a long corridor, the devil explains that the sailor must choose a room where he will spend eternity.

As they approach the first room, the door opens, and the sailor peers in. There's an endless circle of people standing on hot coals with weights strapped to their backs.

"I don't think I want to spend eternity here," said the sailor.

The devil then showed the sailor the second room.

In this room, the damned walk around on broken glass listening to elevator music.

"This isn't much fun," said the sailor. "I definitely don't want to spend any more time in this room."

In the last room, the sailor was surprised to find the damned standing around up to their armpits in vomit drinking coffee.

"That doesn't look so bad!," said the sailor.
"I'll stay here."

"Very well," said the Devil, closing the door behind him.

"Suddenly, the room supervisor called out on his megaphone: "Alright everybody, coffee break's over. Back on your heads."

What do you call 100 sailors at the bottom of the ocean?

A good start.

Santa Claus, the tooth fairy, an honest sailor and an old drunk are walking down the street together when they simultaneously spot a hundred dollar bill.

Who gets it?

The old drunk, of course. The other three are mythical creatures.

How do you save a drowning sailor?

Throw him a rock.

A rich man who was very close to his money got together with his sailor and two of his friends. He then announced and that he was dying and had less than a month to live.

He handed each person an envelope with $100,000 in it and asked everyone to do him a favor after he died.

"Each of these envelopes contains $100,000," said the rich man. "Since I don't want to go to the afterlife without my money, would you please throw these envelopes into my coffin after I die?"

Every one in the group agreed, and took the envelopes.

About a month later, the rich man died and the group reconvened at the funeral.

As promised, each man threw his envelope into the coffin before it was closed up.

As they were leaving, the first friend said: "I have a confession to make. My local church needed a new altar, so I took $5,000 out of the envelope and bought it."

The next friend looked at his feet and said: "Since we're coming clean, I thought it was a waste of money to bury all of the money in the coffin, so I took $30,000 out of the envelope and bought the hospital a new X-ray machine.

Both men then looked at the sailor, expecting him to also make a confession. "You guys are crooks," said the sailor. "I didn't take any money. I put a check in the coffin for the entire $100,000."

A sailor rang United and asked how long it took to fly from New York to Chicago.

"Just a minute, sir," said the United reservations clerk.

"Thank you," said the sailor and hung up.

A man walked into a bar and asked the barman if he had heard the latest sailor joke.

"I'm warning you," said the sailor loudly, "I'm a sailor who's just working part-time as a sailor to make some extra money."

"That's all right," said the man. "I'll tell it slowly."

A man hired an unemployed sailor as his office assistant. On the first day the phone rang, and the sailor hung up immediately.

"Who was that?," asked the boss.

"Some fool saying it was long distance from Brazil," replied the sailor. "I told him everybody knew that."

What's the difference between a sailor and an onion?

People cry when they cut up an onion.

How do you get a sailor out of a tree?

Cut the rope.

Why do sailors always carry garbage in their pockets?

Identification.

A sailor attended a show where a ventriloquist who fancied himself as a comedian told 20 sailor jokes in a row.

"Look," shouted the sailor, standing up in the audience. "I'm fed up being insulted by all these jokes. Sailors are not as stupid as you make out."

"Sit down," said the ventriloquist. "They're only jokes. Don't tell me that sailors haven't got a sense of humor."

"Be quiet," said the sailor. "I'm not talking to you. "I'm talking to the little fellow on your knee."

A man walks into a bar and says: "I hear sailors are a bunch of hard drinkers. I'll bet $500 to anybody who can drink 20 glasses of whisky back-to-back."

The room is quiet, and no one takes up the man's bet. One person leaves.

Thirty minutes later the person who left returns, and taps the man on the shoulder: "Is your bet still on?," asks the sailor.

"Yes," says the man and as he asks the sailor to line up 20 glasses of whisky. Immediately the sailor tears into all 20 glasses, and drinks them back-to-back.

The other pub patrons cheer as the man hands over the $500 to sailor and says: "Why did you leave the bar before, instead of taking up my challenge when I offered it?"

The sailor said: "$500 is a lot of money, so I went to the bar down the street to see if I could do it first."

What do you call a sailor sitting on the grass?

Fertilizer.

A priest died and went to heaven. When he got there, he found a sailor in line in front of him at the Pearly Gates. Saint Peter came over and said to the priest: "Just a minute, I'll be right back," as he took the sailor away to his room.

A few minutes later he returned and said to the priest: "Follow me to your new quarters."

Along the way, they passed many people in their heavenly abodes, including the sailor's quarters.

The priest was awe-struck by the opulence and splendor of the sailor's quarters. There were fine silks, rare foods and drinks, soft music, and attractive young women to serve him for eternity.

The priest finally arrived at his new quarters—a small 6-foot by 9-foot room with bare walls, a plain bed and a Bible for entertainment. The priest said: "I don't want to sound ungrateful, but how come the sailor gets a magnificent room and I get this dump."

Saint Peter smiled and said: "We have a lot of priests here in heaven, but only one sailor."

Did you hear about the sailor who spent four days in Macy's looking for wheels for a miscarriage?

A sailor and his friend were repairing a barn roof, when suddenly a strong wind blew and knocked their ladder down. Since there was no help nearby, both men decided to jump.

Looking around for something that would break their fall, they saw a pile of manure. The sailor jumped first.

"Are you alright?," asked his friend.

"How deep is it?"

The sailor answers: "I'm fine. It's only up to my knees."

"Great. Here I come," yelled the friend as he lands in a pile of manure up to his neck.

You said it was only up to your knees," cried the friend.

"It did only come up to my knees," said the sailor. "I jumped head first."

Hear the one about the deaf sailor?

Neither did he.

One day a sailor was sitting on a beach when he saw a young woman swimming far out to sea. As he watched, he saw a shark circling her. Immediately, he jumped into the water,

karate chopped the shark, killed it instantly, and helped the young woman swim to the beach.

After he got back to the beach, a journalist ran up to him and said: "That was the most courageous thing I've ever seen. I'm going to let the world know about this. You'll be famous. I can see the headline now: 'Man Saves Girl From Killer Shark.'"

"What do you do for a living?"

"I'm a sailor," replied the man of the moment.

"Great," said the journalist. "You'll see the story in tomorrow's paper."

The next day, the sailor bought the paper and the headline read: "Sailor Kills Girl's Pet."

A young sailor decided to turn his life over to God and thought that the best way to do this was to become a monk, so he checked himself into a monastery.

At his indoctrination the head monk told him that they were sworn to TOTAL silence—but every 10 years they were permitted to speak two words.

After 10 years of total silence, the head monk indicated it was now time for the former sailor to speak his two words.

The monk said: "Bed hard," and then resumed his silent study and work.

Another 10 years passed, and the head monk again indicated it was time for him to speak his two words.

The monk said: "Food bad," and the former sailor then resumed his silent study and work.

Thirty years after entering the monastery, it was again time for the former sailor to speak, this time he said:
"I quit."

The head monk shook his head and said: "I knew this was coming. You've done nothing but complain for the past 30 years!"

Did you hear about the sailor who was asked to be a Jehovah's Witness?

He refused because he didn't see the accident.

A sailor went to his doctor and said he had a serious problem because he could never remember what he said.

"When did you first notice this problem?," asked the doctor.

"What problem?," asked the sailor.

A sailor was jumping up and down on the floor yelling and screaming when a friend walked into the room.

"What's wrong?," asked the friend.

"Nothing, nothing at all," relied the sailor. "I'm just so happy. I finished a jigsaw puzzle in record time."

"How long did it take you?, asked the friend."

"Six months," replied the sailor. "On the box it said three to five years."

Not all sailors are bad, but it's a crying shame that the other ninety-nine percent make the rest look bad.

A drunk climbs on a bar stool in a bar and screams: "All sailors are thieves."

A man stands up and says: "I resent that remark."

The drunk shouts back: "Are you a sailor?" "No," says the man "I'm a thief."

A sailor and his wife in their 60s were visited by a fairy who granted them both a wish.

"I want to travel round the world with my darling husband," said the sailor's wife.

Two tickets for a luxury cruise magically appeared in her hand.

A couple of minutes later the sailor said: "Sorry, but my wish is to have a wife 30 years younger than me."

The fairy waved her wand, and suddenly he was 92.

Did you hear about the sailors' Rubik's cube?

It's white on all sides and it takes two seconds to solve.

A sailor went to a pet shop and asked how many budgie birds were in stock. "We have 99 birds," replied the shop owner. "I'll take them all," said the sailor. He went to a tailor and had 99 pockets sewn into his jacket. He then put a budgie bird in each pocket and went up to the top of the tallest building in town and jumped off.

The sailor hit the ground with an almighty smack and lay there groaning until a person passed by and asked him what had happened. "I don't know," replied the sailor. "But that's the last time I try budgie jumping."

Two sailors were walking home one night after drinking when a severed head rolled along the ground in front of them.

The first sailor picked it up, and asked if it was their good friend Mike. "No," said the second sailor: "Mike was taller than that."

An unemployed sailor got a job at a sawmill. Just before lunch, he yelled: "Dave, I lost my finger."

"How did you do it?," asked Dave.

"I just touched this big spinning thing here, like thi...," replied the sailor.

"Darn! There goes another one!," yelled the sailor.

How do you brainwash a sailor?

Give him an enema.

A sailor opened her morning newspaper and was dumbfounded to read in the obituary column that her best friend Susan had died. Before she could do anything, the phone rang. It was Susan.

"Did you see my obituary in today's newspaper?," asked Susan. "It said I died!!"

"Of course I saw it," replied the sailor. "Where are you calling from?"

What do you have when a sailor is buried up to his neck in sand?

Not enough sand.

A sailor was staggering home after a hard night of drinking with a bottle of wine in his back pocket when he slipped and fell badly. Struggling to his feet, the sailor felt something wet running down his leg.

"Please, God," implored the sailor, "let it be blood!"

A sailor went to trial for armed robbery when the jury foreman came out and announced: "Not guilty."

"That's great," shouted the sailor.

"Does that mean I can keep the money?," the sailor asked the sailor.

What does a sailor say when you blow in his ear?

"Thanks for the refill!"

A sailor phoned the maternity ward. "Quick," he said. "Send an ambulance, my wife is having a baby!"

"Tell me, is this her first baby?," the doctor asked.

"No, this is her husband Kevin," replied the sailor.

A sailor and his friend were catching the subway late one night when they came across a notice stating: "Dogs Must Be Carried On the Escalator."

"Great," said the sailor to his friend. "Where am I going to find a dog at this time of night?"

Two mothers were bragging about their sons.

The first said: "My son is such a saint. He studied hard, got himself a degree, doesn't smoke, and he hasn't so much as looked at a woman in over two years."

The sailor's mother responds: "My son is also quite a saint. He studied hard, became a sailor and not only hasn't he not looked at a woman in more than three years, but he hasn't touched any liquor in all that time."

"My word," said the first mother. "You must be so proud."

"I am," said the sailor's mother. "And, when he gets out of jail, I'm going to throw him a huge party."

Sailor: "My dog fell down a hole and I had to shoot it."

Friend: "Did you shoot it in the hole?"

Sailor: "No, in the head."

A sailor, wanting to earn some money, decided to hire herself out as a handyman and started canvassing a wealthy neighborhood.

She went to the front door of the first house and asked the owner if he had any jobs for her to do.

"Well, you can paint my porch," replied the homeowner. "How much will you charge?"

The sailor said, "How about $50?"

The homeowner agreed and told her that the paint and ladders were in the garage.

The homeowner's wife heard the conversation and asked her husband: "Does she realize that the porch goes all the way around the house?"

"She should," said the homeowner. "She was on the porch."

A short time later, the sailor came to the door to collect her money.

"You're finished already?," the homeowner asked.

"Yes," the sailor answered. "Since I had some paint left over, I decided to give it two coats."

Impressed, the homeowner reached in his pocket for the $50.

"And by the way," the sailor added, "It's not a Porch, it's a Ferrari."

What do you call a sailor with two brain cells?

Pregnant.

Two sailors won $5,000,000 in a lottery. While having a drink one night, the first sailor said to the second sailor:

"What are we going to do about the begging letters?"

The second sailor said:

"We're going to continue sending them out?"

Hear about the sailor who got stuck in a bear trap?

Chewed off both arms and one leg and still couldn't get away.

A broke sailor decides to ask God for help.

"Dear Lord," he prays. "If I don't get some cash, I'm going to lose everything. Please let me win the lottery."

Lottery night comes, but the sailor doesn't win.

He prays even harder, saying: "God, why have you forsaken me? My children are starving. Please just let me win."

Suddenly there is a blinding flash of light, and the sailor hears God speak.

"Work with me on this," God says. "Buy a ticket."

How do you keep a sailor happy in his old age?

Tell him jokes when he's young.

A sailor walks into a doctor's office and tells the doctor she's broken every single bone in her body.

"That's impossible," says the doctor.

The sailor says: "It's true. Look!" She then touches her leg with her index finger and screams: "Ouch!"

Then she touches her arm and yells: "Eeeeoooow!"

Finally she touches her ribs and can barely maintain her composure as the tears start to roll down her face.

"See, I told you I broke every bone in my body," she said.

The doctor rubs his chin, then conducts a thorough examination.

"Well, Miss," he tells her, "I've got some good news and some bad news. The good news is, you haven't broken every bone in your body. The bad news is, you've broken your finger."

The sailor was interviewing a sailor for a position in his company. He wanted to find out something about her personality so he asked: "If you could have a conversation with someone, living or dead, who would it be?"

The sailor quickly responded, "The living one."

How do you tell who the sailor is on an oil drilling platform?

He's the one throwing bread to the helicopters.

Did you hear about the sailor who took a roll of toilet paper to a crap game?

"So, have you figured what to buy your wife for the holidays?," asked Sam.

"I sure have," replied the sailor.

"My wife made it easy. She said she wanted something with diamonds, so I bought her a deck of cards."

A sailor returned home from work early one day and found his wife in bed with another man.

Upset, he grabbed his gun and pointed it at his head, which made his wife burst out laughing.

"What are you laughing at," cried the sailor.
"You're next.

How many sailors does it take to screw in a light bulb?

How many can you afford?

An unemployed sailor and his wife moved to a
farm to reduce costs and work out what to do while the
economy recovered. Their modest house had no running water
or electricity.

Nine months after they moved, the sailor's wife's water broke
and the doctor arrived.

"What do you want me to do, doctor?," asked the
sailor.

"Hold the lantern. Here it comes," said the doctor as he held
up child for all to see.

"Congratulations, you're the proud father of a ...," said the
doctor.

Before he could finish his sentence, the doctor said: "Wait a
minute. Hold the lantern," and the doctor delivered a beautiful
baby daughter to the sailor and his wife.

A couple of minutes later he again shouted: "Hold the lantern,"
and moments later held up a third baby.

"Doctor," asks the sailor, "Do you think it's the light that's
attracting them?"

A cop pulls over two sailors who were very, very
drunk.

He says to the first: "What is your name and address?"

The sailor replies: "I'm Mark Johnstone of no fixed address."

The cop turns to the second sailor, and asks the same question.

"I'm David Harris, and I live in the apartment above Mark."

A drunk sailor gets on a bus and asks the conductor how long the trip is between New York and Boston.

"About four hours, depending on traffic," said the driver.

"Okay," says the drunk. "How long is the trip between Boston and New York?"

The dog driver says to the sailor: "It's still about four hours. Why do you think there'd be a difference?"

"Well," says the drunk sailor: "It's only a week between Christmas and New Year, but it's a lot longer between New Year and Christmas!"

How do you save a drowning sailor?

Take your foot off his head.

Why did the sailor put dynamite in his trunk?

In case he needed to blow up his tires.

A sailor and his two friends were about to go down the waterslide when a wrinkled old man steps in front of them.

"This is a magic ride," says the wrinkled old man. "You will land in whatever you shout out on the way down."

"I'm game," said the first friend and shouted "Gold," at the top of his voice as he slid down the slide. When he hit the bottom he found himself surrounded by thousands of gold coins.

The next friend shouted "Silver" at the top of her voice, and landed in more silver coinage than she knew what to do with.

The sailor went last and, launching himself from the top of the slide shouted "weeee!"

Why do they bury sailors 20 feet deep after they die?

Because deep down they are really nice people.

How do you get a sailor to climb on the roof of a bar?

Tell him drinks are on the house!

A sailor lived with his dog for many years, and when the dog died, he went to his local parish priest and asked if services could be said for his dog.

The priest said: "No, we can't have services for a dog here, but that new church down the street that might be willing to do it."

"Thank you," said the sailor. "Do you think $50,000 is a big enough donation?"

"Why didn't you tell me the dog was Catholic?," said the priest.

What's the difference between sailors and pigs?

Pigs don't turn into sailors when they drink.

A sailor had just finished reading a book titled, You Can Be The Man of Your House."

He stormed into the kitchen and said to his wife: "From now on, you need to know that I am the man of this house and my word is law. You will prepare me a gourmet meal tonight, and when I'm done eating, you'll serve me a scrumptious dessert.

And, after dinner, you're going to go upstairs with me and we will have the kind of sex that I want. "Then, you're going to draw me a bath, wash my back and towel me dry and bring me my robe. Then, you'll massage my feet and hands. Then tomorrow, guess who's going to dress me and comb my hair?"

The sailor's wife replied: "The funeral director?"

What's the difference between a sailor and a computer?

You only have to punch information into a computer once.

Did you hear about the sailor who studied all night for his blood test.

Why do sailors hate M&Ms?

They're too hard to peel.

What do you call a sailor who scores well in an IQ test?

A cheat.

There was a sailor who worked hard all his life and saved all of his money, refusing to part with any of it except for essentials.

On his deathbed, the sailor turned to his wife and said: "When I die, I want you to take all my money and put it in the casket with me so I take it to afterlife with me."

His wife faithfully promised to carry out his last wish and agreed to put all of his money into the casket with him.

At the funeral, the service was held and just before they closed the casket, his wife shouted: "Wait a moment, and quickly put a metal box in the casket next to the sailor. The undertaker closed the casket down and rolled it away.

The wife's friend turned to her and said: "Girl, I knew you weren't foolish enough to put all of his money in the coffin, what was in the box?"

The sailor's wife replied: I promised to put his money in the casket and I can't go back on my word.

"You mean to tell say, you me you put all of his money in the coffin?," said the friend.

"You bet I did," said the sailor's wife. "I withdrew all his money from his bank account, put it in my checking account and wrote him a check. If he can cash it, then he can spend it."

A sailor is someone who thinks the three major political parties are Republican, Democratic and Cocktail.

A sailor walks into the bar and says to the sailor: "I'll bet you $200 I can pee into that glass on the top shelf without spilling a drop."

The sailor contemplates this and says: "You're on."

So the sailor drops his pants and pees all over the bar. When he's finished the only dry spot left is the top shelf.

The sailor is beside himself with laughter, but stops laughing when he sees the sailor laughing his head off.

"Why are you laughing?," he asks the sailor, "You've just lost $200."

"Yes," said the sailor. "I did lose $200, but I bet the guys outside $1,000 that I could pee all over your bar and you'd be laughing."

Why do sailors drive BMWs?

Because they can't spell Porsche.

A sailor boards a plane to New York with a ticket for the economy section. She looks at the seats in economy and then looks into the front cabin at the first-class seats.

Seeing that the first-class seats are larger and more comfortable, the sailor takes the last empty one.

The flight attendant checks her ticket and asks the sailor to move back to her seat in economy.

The sailor refuses.

Flustered, the flight attendant goes to the cockpit and informs the captain of the problem.

The captain goes back and tells the woman that her assigned seat is in economy.

The sailor again refuses to move.

The captain doesn't want to cause a commotion, and so he returns to the cockpit to discuss the problem with the copilot.

The copilot says that his girlfriend is a sailor, and that he can take care of the problem.

He then goes back and briefly whispers something in the sailor's ear.

She immediately gets up, says: "Thank you so much," hugs the copilot, and rushes back to her seat in economy.

The sailor and flight attendant, who were watching with rapt attention, together ask the copilot what he had said to the sailor.

He replies, "I just told her that the first class section wasn't going to New York."

What do you call a fly in a sailor's head?

Space invader.

A man gets a call from his sailor friend.

"I've got a problem," says the sailor.

"What's the matter?," asks the friend.

"Well, I've bought this jigsaw puzzle, but it's too hard. None of the pieces fit together and I can't find any edges," said the sailor.

"What's the picture of?," asks the friend.

"It's of a big rooster," replies the sailor.

"All right," says the friend. "I'll come over and have a look."

As he gets to the sailor's house, he goes into the kitchen and finds the pieces on the kitchen table.

The friend looks at the jigsaw and then turns to the sailor and says: "For Pete's sake—put the cornflakes back in the box."

Why do sailors' lunchboxes have clear lids?

So they can tell if it's morning or afternoon.

A sailor goes to Australia for a vacation. There he meets an Aussie farmer and gets talking.

The Aussie shows off his wheat field and the sailor says: "Oh! We have wheat fields that are twice as large."

Then they walk around the farm and the Aussie shows off his herd of cattle.

The sailor immediately says: "We have longhorns that are at least twice as large as your cows."

The conversation has almost died when the sailor sees a herd of kangaroos hopping through the field.

The sailor asks: "And what are those?"

The Aussie gives the sailor an incredulous look
and asks: "Don't you have any grasshoppers where you come from?"

What's the difference between yoghurt and a sailor?

Yoghurt has a little culture.

What's a sailor's idea of safe sex?

Locking the car doors.

Did you hear about the sailor who saw a notice reading: "Man wanted for Robbery and Murder?"

He went in and applied for the job.

One night a police officer saw a sailor looking for something under a street light. He asked him if he had lost something there.

The sailor said: "I lost my keys in the alley."

"Why are you looking under the light," asked the police officer.

The sailor responded: "It's a lot easier to look over here."

The circus owner puts an ad in the newspaper for a part-time, trainee lion tamer.

A sailor thinks it's an easy way to make some extra money, so he applies and gets the job.

"What do I do?," asks the sailor.

"Simply hold the chair, the lion will obey," said the circus owner.

"And what should I do if the lion doesn't obey?," asked the sailor.

"Crack the whip," said the circus owner."

"And if that doesn't work?," asked the sailor.

"You have a revolver. Shoot it into the air," said the circus owner."

"And if that doesn't work, what do I do then?," asked the sailor.

"Well then, throw shit at the lion," said the circus owner who was growing tired on this line of questioning."

"Where do I get that from?," asked the sailor.

"Trust me on that," said the circus owner. "You'll have plenty!"

Have you heard about the sailor who cheated Amtrak?

He bought a round-trip ticket to Washington and didn't go back.

An out-of-work sailor was given the job of painting the lines down the middle of a highway. On his first day, he painted six miles; the next day three miles; the following day less than a mile.

The boss came up to him and said: "Your productivity is dropping rapidly. If you don't pick up your game, I'm going to have to let you go."

The sailor replied: "I just can't do any better. Each day I keep getting farther away from the paint can."

What's the difference between a puppy and sailor?

If you put a puppy in a room by itself for an hour, it'll eventually stop whining.

A man died and was taken to his place of eternal torment by the devil. As he passed sulfurous pits and shrieking sinners, he saw a man he recognized as his sailor snuggling up to a beautiful woman.

"That's unfair!," he cried. "I have to roast for all eternity, and my sailor gets to spend his afterlife with a beautiful woman."

"Shut up!," barked the devil, jabbing him with his pitchfork. "Who are you to question that woman's punishment?"

What's wrong with sailor jokes?

Sailors don't think they're funny, and nobody else thinks they're jokes.

What is the difference between a catfish and a sailor?

One is a scum sucking bottom dweller and the other is a fish.

Two sailors went into a bar and ordered two drinks. They pulled out their lunch from their briefcases and started to eat.

The waiter became quite concerned and marched over and said: "You can't eat your own sandwiches in here!"

The sailors looked at each other, shrugged their shoulders and then exchanged sandwiches.

Why is it good to have a sailor as a passenger?

Because you can park in the handicapped zone.

"If there are any idiots in the room, will they please stand up," said the sailor giving a lecture.

After a long silence, one attendee rose to his feet.

"Now," asked the sailor. "Why do you consider yourself an idiot?"

"Well, actually I don't," replied the attendee. "But I hate seeing you standing up here all by yourself."

What do UFOs and smart sailors have in common?

You hear about them all the time but you never see one.

How can you tell if a sailor made the chocolate chip cookies?

There are M&Ms shells on the floor.

A successful sailor parked his brand new Porsche in front of the office to show it off to his colleagues. As he got out, a truck came along too close to the curb and completely tore off the driver's side.

The sailor immediately called 911 and in less than 5 minutes the law arrived. Before the police officer could ask any questions, the sailor started screaming about how his brand-new car would never be the same again.

After the sailor had finished his rant, the police officer shook his head in disbelief.

"I can't believe how materialistic you sailors are," he said. "You're so focused on your possessions you don't notice anything else."

"How can you say that?," asked the sailor.

The police officer replied: "Haven't you noticed that your left arm is missing from your elbow down? It was torn off when the truck hit you."

The sailor looked down in absolute horror and screamed: "Where's my Rolex?"

Then there was a female sailor who went swimming off the coast of Hawaii because she heard they were man-eating sharks.

Did you hear about the sailor who wore a glove on one hand?

The forecaster said: "Tomorrow may be hot, but on the other hand, it could be cold."

A sailor was on vacation and was told about a great restaurant in town, but thought it was closed because the sign in the window said: "Home Cooking."

A sailor went into a bar with burnt feet. The barman said: "How did you burn your feet?"

The sailor said: "Cooking spaghetti."

"How on earth can you burn your feet cooking spaghetti?," asked the astonished barman.

"Easy," said the sailor. "I just followed the instructions. They said: Pierce top of can and stand in boiling water."

A sailor went to a baseball game with a friend, but got stuck in traffic and arrived after the fifth inning. When they arrived, the score was still zero-zero.

"Oh good," said the sailor, we haven't missed anything.

What do you call 16 sailors standing in a room around a beer keg?

A dope ring.

Did you hear about the two not-so-bright sailors who tried to make money selling watermelons?

They bought a truckload of melons for $5.00 each, and sold them for $5.00 each.

At the end of the day they sold everything they had bought, but couldn't work out why they had exactly the same amount of money as when they started.

"This isn't working," said one sailor. "We're not making any money. What are we going to do?"

The other sailor replied: "I guess we're going to have to get a bigger truck."

What's does a sailor make for dinner?

Reservations.

A sailor ordered a pizza. "Do you want it cut into four or eight slices?," asked the pizza maker.

The sailor replied: "Better make it four, I'm not very hungry."

A sailor went to the doctor and asked how to have a better sex life. The doctor said: "Run five miles a day."

A week later the doctor called and said: "How is your sex life?"

The sailor said: "I don't know, I'm 35 miles from home."

Did you hear about the sailor who wore two jackets when he painted his house?

The instructions on the can said: "Put on two coats."

Why do sailors laugh three times when they hear a joke?

Once when it is told, once when it is explained to them, and once when they understand it.

How do you make a sailor's eyes light up?

Shine a flashlight in their ear.

Two sailors rented a boat to go fishing in their local lake. Amazed at the number of fish they caught, they decided to come back the next day to try their luck again.

The first sailor asked: "How will we find this spot again?"

The second sailor takes a can of spray paint, paints an X on the bottom of the boat, and says: "We'll just look for this X tomorrow."

The first sailor said: "You idiot! How do you know we'll get the same boat?"

Did you hear about the Buddhist sailor who refused Novocaine during a root canal? The goal: transcend dental medication.

A priest was seated next to a sailor on a flight to Texas. After the plane took off, the sailor ordered a gin and tonic, which was brought and placed before him.

The flight attendant then asked the preacher if he wanted a drink.

Appalled, the preacher said: "I'd rather be tied up and taken advantage of by women of ill-repute, rather than let liquor touch my lips."

The sailor then handed his drink back to the attendant and said: "Me too, I didn't know we had a choice."

How can you tell if a sailor has been using the computer?

There's Wite-out on the screen.

Did you hear about the sailor who turned up at a friend's house in a wet shirt?

The label said wash and wear.

During a visit to the doctor, a sailor asks: "How do you determine whether a person should be put in an insane asylum?"

"The doctor said: "We fill up a bathtub and offer the person a teaspoon, cup and a bucket and ask them to empty the tub."

"I understand," said the sailor. "A normal person would use the bucket because it's bigger than the spoon or the teacup."

"No," said the doctor. "A normal person would pull the plug. Do you want a bed near the window or the door?"

How can you be sure that Santa is a sailor?

Every house has at least one door and window and Santa still chooses to come in through the chimney.

Did you hear about the sailor who became a loan shark?

Lent out all his money and skipped town.

Why did the sailor cut off all his fingers?

So he could write shorthand.

Two sailors were adrift in a lifeboat. While rummaging through the boat's provisions the first sailor found a rusty old lamp.

He rubs the lamp and a genie suddenly appears. "Thank you for freeing me," said the genie. "Due to the current economic situation and the cutbacks, I can only grant you one wish.

"That's OK," replied the first sailor. "All I want you to do is turn the entire ocean into beer."

The genie clapped his hands with a deafening crash, and suddenly the entire sea became beer.

The genie disappeared, and only the gentle lapping of beer on the hull broke the stillness as the two sailors considered their circumstances.

"Nice going," said the second sailor. "Now we're going to have to pee in the boat."

A sailor checked into a room at his hotel and asked the lady at the registration desk if the porn channel in his room was disabled.

"No, it's regular porn, you sick bastard," replied the desk clerk.

The Personalized Edition

If you'd like to make this book your own, why not order a personalized copy for yourself or a friend. Simply go to www.dolyttle.com or www.thebesteverbook.com and enter your information. And we'll send you your very own copy of The Best Ever Book of YOUR NAME Jokes.

But the value doesn't end there. Not only will we put your name and picture on the cover and throughout the book, we'll also include one of your friends in the jokes so you can make fun of them.

At $19.95 per copy it's a great deal. If you're scared of the Internet, simply fill in the attached form and we'll do the rest.

ORDER! FORM

Dolyttle & Seamore
198 Garth Road Suite 2D
Scarsdale, NY 10583
212-496-8771 • info@dolyttle.com
(For faster service go to www.dolyttle.com)

Name _____

Address _____ Apt. ____

City _____ State _____ ZIP _____

Country _____

Email _____

Phone _____

Title: The Best Ever Book of _____ Jokes

Friend's Name _____

If you don't have a friend, don't worry about it. We'll nominate somebody be your friend, at absolutely no additional cost. Each book is $19.95 plus $3.99 shipping for the first book and $2.00 for each additional copy. Call for pricing for large orders and corporate prices.

WWW.DOLYTTLE.COM

Occupations

Account executive, Accountant, Acupuncturist, Actor, Administrative Assistant, Administrator, Aide, Air traffic controller, Ambulance officer, Analyst, Anesthesiologist, Announcer, Antique dealer, Architect, Assistant, Astronomer, Athlete, Audiologist, Auditor, Author, Baggage handler, Balloon artist, Banker, Baptist, Barber, Bartender, Beautician, Bee keeper, Benefit manager, Bill collector, Biologist, Bodybuilder, Book keeper, Boy scout, Breeder, Bricklayer, Builder, Building manager, Bus driver, Butcher, Camera operator, Camp counselor, Candy store owner, Car dealer, Caregiver, Carpenter, Carpet layer, Cartographer, Catholic, Chauffeur, Chef, Chemical engineer, Chemist, Chiropractor, Cinematographer, Civil engineer, Civil servant, Claim adjuster, Clerk, clown, Communist, Company director, Compliance officer, Computer engineer, Computer operator, Computer programmer, Conductor, Conference producer, Congressman, Conservationist, Cook, Copy editor, Courier, Criminal, Dancer, Data entry, Data entry clerk, Dealer, Debt collector, Deli owner, Delivery person, Democrat, Dental assistant, Dental hygienist, Dermatologist, Designer, Detailer, Detectives, Dispatcher, Doctor, Dog Walker, Doorman, Dressmaker, Drug dealer, Dry cleaner, Economist, Editor, Electrician, Emergency Medical Technician, Engineer, Engraver, Entertainer, Entrepreneur, Environmental engineer, Epidemiologist, Executive, Exporter, Farmer, Fencer, Fire fighter, Fisher man, Flight engineer, Food scientist, Food technologist, Fundraiser, Funeral director, Furniture maker, Garbage collector, Gardener, Geographer, Geologist, Girl scout, Golfer, Grave digger, Grocer, Guard, Guide, Hairdresser, Handyman, Hardware store owner, Hat maker, Hiring manager, Historian, Horticulturist, Host, Hostess, HR manager, Importer, Industrial engineer, Information system manager, Inspector, Instructor, Insurance agent, Interpreter, Janitor, Jew, Jeweler, Journalist, Judge, Laborer, Landscaper, Laundry assistant, Law clerk, Lawyer, Librarian, Life guard, Locksmith, Machinist, Magician, Mail sorter, Makeup artist, Manager, Managing director, Manicurist, Marketing manager, Marriage counselor, Mathematician, Meat slicer, Medical assistant, Messenger, Meter reader, Meteorologist, Midwife, Miner, Minister, Model, Motor cycle, Muslim, Naturopath, Norman, Nuclear engineer, Nurse, Nursing aide, Obstetrician, Occupational ther apist, Optician, Optometrist, Orthodontist, Paralegal, Parking inspector, Party planner, Pattern maker, Payroll clerk, Performer, Personnel manager, Pest control, Pharmacist, Pharmacy aide, Philosopher, Photographer, Physician, Physical ther apist, Physicist, Pilot, Pipe layer, Pizza parlor owner, Plumber, Podiatrist, Police officer, Political scientist, Politician, Porter, Postal worker, Postmaster, Potter, PR professional, President, Priest, Printer, Prison guard, Private detectives, Producer, Professor, Programmer, Projectionist, Proofreader, Psychiatric nurse, Psychologist, Purchasing manager, Rabbi, Radiographer, Real estate agent, Receptionist, Referee, Refrigeration mechanic, Registrar, Repairman, Reporter, Republican, Rigger, Roofer, Runner, Sailor, Sales manager, Sales rep, Salesperson, Scientist, Secretary, Security guard, Senator, Sher iff, Shoe maker, Sign writer, Singer, Skier, Skin care specialist, Small business owner, Social worker, Socialist, Sociologist, Soldier, Sound technician, Speech ther apist, Spy, Statistician, Student, Superintendent, Supervisor, Surgeon, Surveillance officer, Surveyor, Swimmer, Swimming instructor, Tailor, Sailor, Teaching assistant, Technician, Technologist, Technology writer, Telemarketer, Tennis player, Ther apist, Ticket collector, Title examiner, Tour guide, Travel agent, Truck driver, Tutor, Tire dealer, Umpire, Underwriter, Upholsterer, Urban planner, Urologist, Usher, Veterinarian, Waiter, Waitress, Web designer, Welder, Window washer, Woodworkers, Writer, Zookeeper, Zoologist..

Nationalities

Afghan, Albanian, Algerian, American, Andorran, Angolan, Anguillan, Antiguan, Barbadian, Argentine, Armenian, Australian, Austrian, Azerbaijani, Bahamian, Bahraini, Bangladeshi, Barbadian, Belarusian, Belgian, Belizean, Beninese, Bermudian, Bhutanese, Bolivian, Bosnian , Batswana, Brazilian, British, Bruneian, Bulgarian, Burkinabe, Burmese, Burundian, Cambodian, Cameroonian, Canadian, Cape Verdian, Caymanian, Central African, Chadian, Chilean, Chinese, Christmas Islander, Cocos Islander, Colombian, Comoran, Congolese, Costa Rican, Croat, Cuban, Cypriot, Czech, Dane, Djibouti, Dominica, Dutch, East Timorese, Ecuadorean, Egyptian, Emirati, Equatoguinean, Eritrean, Estonian, Ethiopian, Falkland Islander, Fijian, Filipino, Finnish, French, Gabonese, Gambian, Georgian, German, Ghanaian, Gibraltarian, Greek, Greenlander, Grenadian, Guadeloupian, Guatemalan, Guinean, Guinea-Bissauan, Guianese, Guyanese, Haitian, Herzegovinian, Honduran, Hungarian, Icelander, Indian, Indonesian, Iranian, Iraqi, Irish, Israeli, Italian, Jamaican, Japanese, Jordanian, Kazakhstani, Kenyan, Kiribati, Kittian, Kiwi, Korean, Kuwaiti, Kyrgyzstani, Laotian, Latvian, Lebanese, Liberian, Libyan, Liechtensteiner, Lithuanian, Luxembourger, Macedonian, Madagascan, Malagasy, Malawian, Malaysian, Maldivian, Malian, Maltese, Marshallese, Martinican, Mauritanian, Mauritian, Mahorais, Mexican, Micronesian, Moldovan, Monacan, Mongolian, Montserratian, Moroccan, Montenegrin, Mozambican, Myanmarese, Namibian, Nauruan, Nepalese, Netherlander, New Zealander, Nicaraguan, Niger, Nigerien, Nigerian, Norwegian, Omani, Pakistani, Palauan, Palestinian, Panamanian, Papua New Guinean, Paraguayan, Peruvian, Polish, Portuguese, Puerto Rican, Qatari, Reunionese, Romanian, Russian, Rwandan, Saint Helenian, Nevisian, Saint Lucian, Saint Vincentian, Salvadoran, Sammarinese, Sao Tomean, Saudi Arabian, Scottish, Senegalese, Serbian, Seychellois, Sierra Leonean, Singaporean, Slovak, Slovene, Solomon Islander, Somalian, Somali, South African, Spaniard, Sri Lankan, Sudan, Sudanese, Surinamer, Swazi, Swedish, Swiss, Syrian, Taiwanese, Tajik, Tanzanian, Thai, Tobagonian, Togolese, Tongan, Trinidadian, Tunisian, Turkish, Turkmen, Tuvaluan, Ugandan, Ukrainian, Uruguayan, Uzbekistani, Vanuatu, Venezuelan, Vietnamese, Virgin Islander, Welsh, Yemeni, Zambian, Zimbabwean.

Sports

Adventure, Archery, Athletics, Badminton, Baseball, Basketball, Bowling, Boxing, Canoe, Cricket, Cycling, Diving, Equestrian, Fencing, Football, Golf, Gymnastics, Handball, Hockey, Jockey, Kayak, Martial Arts, , Mountaineering, Netball, Orienteering, Ping Pong, Polo, Racing, Rowing, Rugby, Sailing, Shooting, Soccer, Softball, Surfing, Swimming, Table Tennis, Volleyball, Weightlifting, Wresting.

Religion

Atheist, Buddhist, Christian, Catholic, Protestant, Unitarian, Baptist, Jewish, Confucianist, Hare Krishna, Hindi, Muslim, Jehovah's Witness, Mormon, Rastafarian, Scientologist, Seventh-day Adventist, Sikh, Pagan, Witch.

Political Parties

Communist, Conservative, Democrat, Independent, Labour, Liberal, Libertarian, Non-Voter, Republican, Socialist, Tea Party.

Or

Write Your own

The Best Ever Guide to _____ Jokes

Lots and Lots of Jokes Specially Repurposed for _____

Visit www.dolyttle.com to find out more.

Printed in Great Britain
by Amazon.co.uk, Ltd.,
Marston Gate.